Amber comes into Archie's bedroom.

"Come on, Archie," she says.
"You're going to have so much fun
on your first day at school!"

"Is it time for school yet, Mummy?" asks Archie.

"No," says Mummy.
"You have to eat up all
your breakfast first.
You're going to have
a busy day."

Mummy puts a water bottle and some fruit in Archie's school bag.

"Can Bunny come too?" asks Archie.

"Yes," says Mummy.
"But take care of him."

They set off for school. Archie follows Amber, with Mummy close behind.

"Stop, Archie!" calls Mummy. "You've dropped Bunny!"

They arrive at school and Amber goes to
her classroom. Archie meets his teacher.
Her name is Miss Whimsie.

Miss Whimsie holds Archie's hand
and they say goodbye to Mummy.

"Which coat peg would you like?"
asks Miss Whimsie.

"Please can I have the
apple?" asks Archie.
"I love apples."

"You will be sitting at the red table, Archie," says Miss Whimsie.

He sits down and soon makes a friend called Breeze.

"What's your bunny's name?" asks Breeze.

"Bunny," says Archie.

Miss Whimsie shows the children all
the fun activities to do in the classroom.

"Archie, you and Breeze can
start on the craft table."

Miss Whimsie helps Archie
to make a rocket.

"Zoom!" Archie makes the rocket
fly and knocks paint over Bunny.

"Oh dear," says Archie.

"Never mind," says Miss Whimsie.

It is soon snack time.

Whoops!

Archie spills his milk all over Bunny.

"Oh dear,"
says Archie.

"Never mind," says
Miss Whimsie.

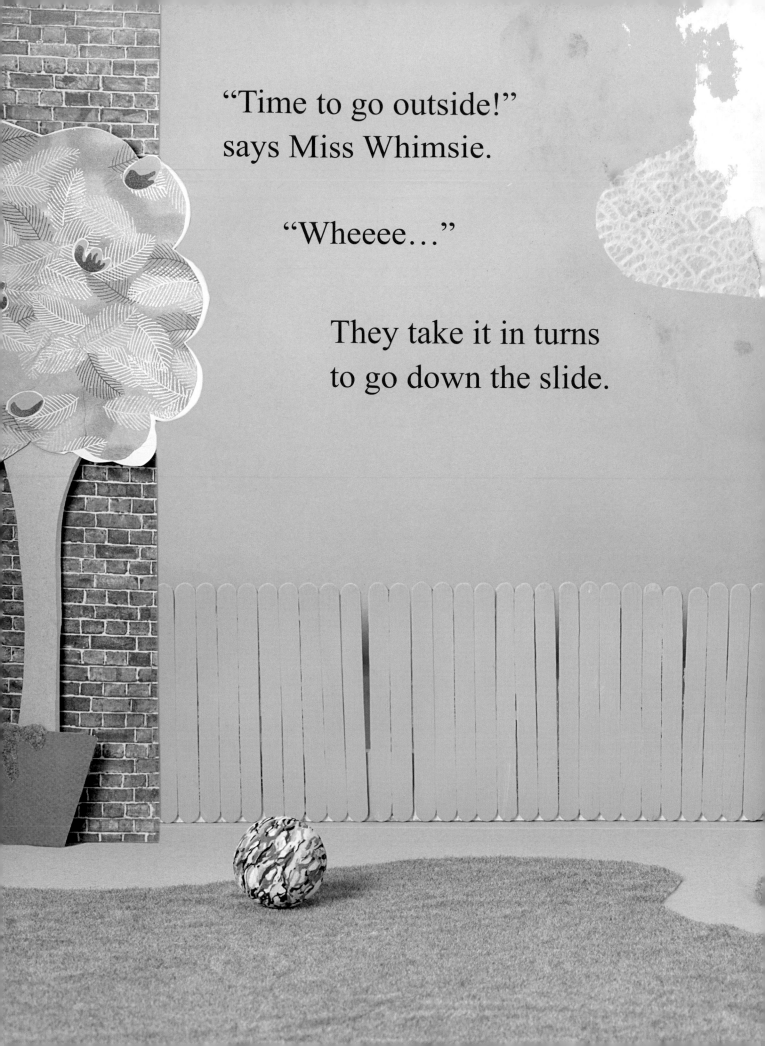

"Time to go outside!"
says Miss Whimsie.

"Wheeee…"

They take it in turns
to go down the slide.

Next Archie plays in the sandpit.

Bunny gets buried in the sand.

"Oh dear," says Breeze.

"Never mind," says Archie. "Bunny is having a bad day, but I'll take care of him."

It's time for lunch.
"Yum!" says Archie.

"Shall I give Bunny some of my sandwich?" asks Breeze

"Thank you, Breeze, but Bunny prefers carrots," says Archie.

In the afternoon, Miss Whimsie
reads a story about dinosaurs.

All the children join in, "Roarrrr!"
Archie holds Bunny close in case he's scared.

At home time, Archie meets Amber.
"School was fun," says Archie. "I want to
come back tomorrow, but Bunny is too little.
He wants to stay at home."